Amazing
Frogs & Toads

WRITTEN BY
BARRY CLARKE

PHOTOGRAPHED BY
JERRY YOUNG

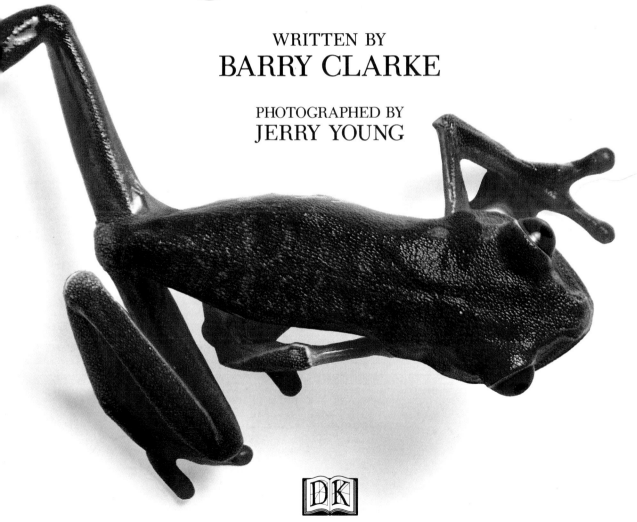

Dorling Kindersley · London

A Dorling Kindersley Book

Project editors Helen Parker and Christine Webb
Art editor Ann Cannings
Managing editor Sophie Mitchell
Editorial director Sue Unstead
Art director Colin Walton

Special photography by Jerry Young
and Jane Burton (page 28)
Illustrations by Ruth Lindsay, Polly Noakes,
and John Hutchinson
Animals supplied by Trevor Smith's Animal World
Editorial consultants The staff of the Natural History Museum, London

The author would like to dedicate this book
to his daughters, Emma and Amy, with love.

First published in Great Britain in 1990 by
Dorling Kindersley Limited
9 Henrietta Street, London WC2E 8PS

Reprinted 1991

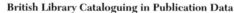

British Library Cataloguing in Publication Data
Clarke, Barry
Amazing frogs and toads
1. Frogs and toads
I. Title
597.8

ISBN 0-86318-473-1

Colour reproduction by Colourscan, Singapore
Typeset by Windsorgraphics, Ringwood, Hampshire
Printed in Italy by A. Mondadori Editore, Verona

Contents

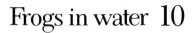

What is a frog?

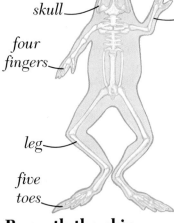

Frogs and toads have short, tubby bodies and large heads with bulging eyes. They have no tail, no fur, feathers, or scales, and no neck. They are amphibians (*am-fib-ee-uns*), which means they can live on land or in water.

skull

arm

four fingers

leg

five toes

Beneath the skin
Frogs have short front legs and long back legs for jumping and swimming.

lungs

heart

Breathing
Like you, frogs have lungs for breathing. But unlike you, they can also breathe through their skin.

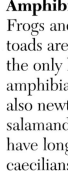

Amphibians
Frogs and toads are not the only kinds of amphibian. There are also newts and salamanders, which have long tails, and caecilians (*se-sill-ee-uns*), which look like big worms.

Newt

Salamander

Caecilian

Most frogs and toads have big eyes so they can see their food – and their enemies!

This frog has smooth, moist skin

Neat feet

Frogs have different feet for different lifestyles. Some have pointed toes, some have sticky toes for climbing, and others have webbed toes for swimming.

digging   climbing   swimming

The oldest singer in town

Insects made the first noises, but the first true song was probably sung by a prehistoric frog.

New discoveries

Many new kinds of frog are found every year. Until 1980 no one knew this little Majorcan midwife toad existed!

Bright eyes

The coloured part of a frog's eye is called the iris (*eye-riss*). It can be deep red, brown, black, green, silver, bronze, or gold. The dark centre, or pupil, isn't always round like yours. Some are triangular, or even heart-shaped!

This toad has dryish, warty skin

Frog or toad?

Frogs usually have smooth, moist skin, while most toads have drier, warty skins. But that is the only difference. They are really all frogs.

Frogs in water

 Most frogs go into the water to lay their eggs in the breeding season. But some spend their whole lives in the water. These are truly aquatic frogs.

Flat frog
The Chilean aquatic bullfrog has a floppy body and long legs – just right for swimming about.

Frog expert
Reading this book is the easy way to learn about frogs. A frog expert, or herpetologist (*her-puh-tol-uh-jist*), spends hours watching and waiting by ponds and lakes, in all kinds of weather.

Hairy frogs?
The "hairs" on this male frog's body are really tiny folds of skin. They help him breathe more easily when he's dashing about during the breeding season.

Chilean aquatic bullfrog
This massive frog spends most of its life in rivers and lakes. It is so greedy it even tries to eat animals almost as big as itself!

Frogman

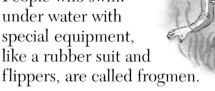

People who swim under water with special equipment, like a rubber suit and flippers, are called frogmen.

Huge tadpoles, small frogs

A paradox is something which seems to be the wrong way around. The paradoxical frog has a huge tadpole which turns into a small frog – not what you would expect at all!

Male singers

When a male frog croaks, its throat acts just like a pump. The skin under its chin blows up like a balloon that may be as big as the frog itself.

Jumping in

Aquatic frogs jump into the water with a loud "plop" when danger approaches.

Burrowing frogs

For many frogs, life is safer under the ground than on top. Here they can hide from hungry enemies but still find plenty to eat themselves. Many frogs, like this narrow-mouthed toad from Malaysia, are master burrowers.

Stony faced
Sitting on the leafy forest floor, this little toad looks just like a slimy wet stone.

Bottom first...
This holy cross toad has a strange way of digging. It shuffles its back legs and then uses the "spades" on its back feet to clear away the soil. Once it has buried itself, it peeps above the ground to spot a passing meal.

Head first...
Some frogs have hard, sharp snouts which they use for burrowing. They push their snouts into the ground, like shovels. Then they use their front legs to dig in – head first.

...Feet last
The spades on the back feet help push the frog's snout into the ground – until it disappears.

Rain frogs

These little frogs only really see the light of day in the rainy season. They spend most of their time in underground tunnels or beneath logs – often sharing their homes with scorpions. No wonder they look so fed up!

Digging with their bare hands

This natterjack toad doesn't need a spade for digging in the sand. His short, stubby fingers with hard tips do the job.

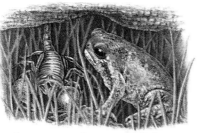

short, strong back legs for burrowing into the soil – bottom first

The mouse, the frog, and the hawk

An old story tells how a frog and a mouse tie their feet together as a sign of friendship. At lunch-time, the frog leaps into the pond to eat and drowns the poor mouse. The mouse's body floats to the top of the water and is soon spotted by a hungry hawk, who picks it up and flies off with a double dinner.

Life in the treetops

Some tree frogs spend their whole lives in the trees, never coming down to the ground. They eat, sleep, find a mate, and even lay their eggs up in the branches or on leaves.

Fighting in the trees

A tree frog's home is its castle. And it's not scared of fighting for its own leaf, branch, or fallen log, either.

big eyes to look out for food – and danger

sticky pads for clinging on

Sunbathing frogs

Frogs need to protect their skin from the sun, just as we do. This South American frog makes a waxy, fatty lotion and wipes it all over its body.

Weather forecast

In Germany, people used to keep green tree frogs in jars with a ladder and some water. They were supposed to climb up or down the ladder as the weather changed. But the poor frogs probably just wanted to get out of the jars!

Sticky feet
Tree frogs have sticky pads on their fingers and toes to help them climb on slippery leaves.

Tree frogs can climb up glass

High jumper
To make sure they land on the right leaf, flying frogs steer in the air with their webbed hands and feet.

Red-eyed tree frog
This Central American frog lays its eggs under leaves that hang over water. As they hatch out, the tadpoles fall into the water below.

Singing in the trees
This little Mexican tree frog is singing to his lady-love – hoping that she will come to his leafy home.

All fingers and toes

As well as living in trees, some tree frogs live in bushes, reeds, and long grass. They climb from leaf to leaf, clinging on with their sticky fingers and toes.

Spring is here!
The tinkling song of the spring peeper is one of the first signs of spring in some parts of America.

Home lovers
In Australia, White's tree frogs often share people's bathrooms.

See-through
The glass frog has strange see-through skin. You can even see this one's heart and insides.

Foam-nesting frogs
Some female tree frogs make a kind of egg white. They beat it into a foam with their back legs and lay their eggs in it. This bubbly nest is dry on the outside but moist inside, where the eggs are.

Leaf-folding frogs
This golden frog lays its eggs on leaves in the water. Then it folds and glues the leaves together to hide the eggs.

Baby-sitting
Male glass frogs watch carefully over their eggs, to keep them from being eaten by other animals. They often rest a hand on the edge of the pile of eggs, though no one really knows why.

White's tree frog
This little Australian frog seems at home on its tree branch. But it doesn't mind visiting people in their homes, either.

Foam birth
When the rains come, the foam-nesting frog's nest becomes runny. The rain-water – and the tadpoles – drip into the water below.

Big mouth, big appetite

Frogs don't eat three meals a day like we do. They eat a lot of food when there's a lot to eat, and they can go for a long time between meals. If they can eat, they will – their next meal might be a long way away!

A frog blinks as it swallows – its eyeballs help force the food down

Sticky tongue
Many frogs and toads have sticky tongues which they can flick out to catch their prey.

Once it has pulled an insect back into its mouth, the frog doesn't stop to chew, but swallows its meal whole.

Chinese eclipse
We now know that eclipses of the moon are caused by the shadow of the earth falling on the moon. But the Chinese once believed they were caused by a three-legged frog who swallowed the moon.

Leap, snap, and it's gone
Frogs often leap out of the water to catch passing insects.

Small frog, big appetite!
A dwarf puddle frog like this one can eat as many as 100 mosquitoes in one night – a big meal for a tiny frog the size of a large peanut!

Gardener's friend
Frogs and toads help protect plants by gobbling up huge numbers of insect pests.

Big frog, big appetite
This ornate horned frog from South America has a huge mouth and can even eat mice and rats. It lies in wait until a tasty meal passes by. In a flash, it leaps up. Two gulps, and the victim has gone!

The croak of some horned frogs sounds like the moo of a cow

19

Not too hot, not too cold

Frogs are cold-blooded, which means that their inside temperature is about the same as the temperature outside. They keep warm by sitting in the sun, and go into the shade or into water to cool off.

A fully grown African bullfrog can give you a nasty bite if you upset it

Dry-weather coat
The African bullfrog digs in underground. It wraps itself in a cocoon, like a papery overcoat, made from old skin. This cocoon stops it drying out when the weather is hot. When the rains come, they seep down, waking up the frog.

Feet in, head down...

If a frog gets hot, it may tuck in its arms, hands, and feet to keep them cool. Oddly enough, it does the same thing in cold weather – this time to keep warm.

Singing in the rain

In hot countries, frogs breed in the rainy season. As soon as the rains begin, the male frogs start croaking wildly to attract partners.

Freezing frogs!

Four kinds of frog can survive the freezing cold of a Canadian winter. They become covered in a blanket of ice, their hearts stop beating, and they even stop breathing.

Water-holding frog

This frog lives in the hot Australian deserts, where it hardly rains. It can store large amounts of water in its body.

Wake me when it's warmer...

Many frogs escape the worst of the winter by hiding under a log or in the mud at the bottom of a pond. Then they go into a kind of deep sleep until spring.

...or when it's colder

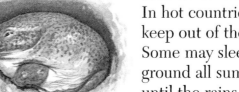

In hot countries, frogs keep out of the heat. Some may sleep underground all summer, until the rains arrive.

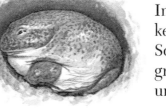

How not to be eaten

Frogs make a tasty meal for many animals. To protect themselves from being eaten, they can hide, pretend to be fierce or frightening, or even make poisons in their skin so that they taste nasty.

Water babies

Frogs that live in puddles, ponds, lakes, and streams often leave only the tops of their heads and eyes showing. If they sense danger, they dive for safety.

Hidden near to a log or stone, this toad is hard to see – until it moves

In hiding

Some frogs blend in perfectly with their surroundings, like this one on its lily pad home.

On tiptoe

A snake could easily gobble up this toad. To frighten it off, the toad puffs itself up and stands on tiptoe so it looks twice as big.

Poison glands

Some toads, like the cane toad, make poison in glands behind their eyes. If a dog tried to pick up the toad, its poison could squirt into the dog's mouth. This would make the dog very ill – it could even die.

Deadly yellow

This dart-poison or poison arrow frog is so poisonous that it shouldn't be touched. One frog's poison can kill 20,000 mice.

Poison pipes

South American Indians use the dart-poison frog's poison for hunting. They put it on the darts for their blowpipes.

Green toads hide during the day and come out at night

I'm an owl and I could eat YOU!

When it's threatened the false-eyed frog hunches over to show two eyespots. To put off braver enemies, a foul-smelling liquid oozes out around the eyespots. If the eyes don't work, the smell should see them off!

Green toad

This handsome toad can puff itself up with air to look bigger, and frighten its enemies.

Hop, skip, and a jump

Frogs can leap away from trouble.

Curious colours

Not *all* frogs are dull brown or grassy green. There are yellow, orange, gold, red, white, and even blue frogs, and some of them are beautifully patterned with many bright colours.

Don't be fooled!

This dart-poison frog looks like a strawberry – but its skin is poisonous.

Warning! You can't eat me!

Bright colours, especially yellows and reds, warn other animals that a frog is not good to eat – or even poisonous. The poison in the skin of these little dart-poison frogs could kill you.

Feeling blue

Some male frogs go blue to attract a female. But this beautiful blue dart-poison frog has a brilliant blue and black pattern all year round.

The tips of the fingers and toes look as if they have been dipped in a red paint pot!

Hidden away
Soldiers wear green and brown clothes so their enemies cannot see them in the fields and forests. This type of clothing is called camouflage.

Now you see me, now you don't
This striped frog from South Africa would easily be seen away from the reeds and tall grasses where it lives. Put it back in its home and it is almost impossible to find.

Light and shade
This little African frog looks just like part of the grass it's sitting on. The light and dark stripes that run down its body match the stripy patterns made by sunlight falling on its reedy home.

wide stripe

narrow stripe

Split in two!
The light lines running down the backs of these two puddle frogs break up their tubby body shape and make them harder to see.

Tricky toad
From above, the oriental fire-bellied toad from China blends in with its leafy background. But when it's disturbed it arches its back and the bottoms of its colourful feet. This quickly scares off hungry enemies.

25

Strange shapes

Not all frogs look like frogs. Some are shaped like leaves, some have small heads, and others have heads that look like a duck's bill. Their strange shapes help the frogs get by wherever they may live.

Big leaf frogs
The Asian leaf frog has flaps of skin (or "horns") over its eyes, and a pointed snout. Its brown skin and jagged shape make it look just like dried leaves on the forest floor.

Helmet head!

This frog's unusual shape helps it blend in with its surroundings. Its oddly-shaped head – prongs at the back, a pointed nose and a very bony skull – looks a bit like a helmet.

Mole or frog?

The Australian mole frog lives in sandy places and in termite mounds. It looks like a mole, with its small head, tiny eyes, and rounded snout. It even digs like a mole – head first, using its strong arms.

Mole frog

Mole

World on his shoulders

People from China and India once believed that the world rested on the back of a giant three-legged frog. But if the frog made the slightest move, it would cause an earthquake.

A duck-billed frog?

The Mexican spoon-headed frog backs into holes in logs and trees. Its bony head fits tightly into the hole, like a cork. This makes it a lot harder for animals to pull it out and make a meal of it.

Little leaf frogs

This little Darwin's frog, with its pointed snout, looks like a green leaf. Having both the right colour and body shape keeps it extra safe.

Frogs and tadpoles

Frogs begin life as eggs. When the eggs hatch, tadpoles swim out. Then the tadpoles slowly turn into small frogs. This amazing change is called metamorphosis *(met-a-mor-foh-sis)*.

1 When a tadpole hatches out of its egg (or frog spawn), it has a round head and body, and a tail. But it has no legs.

2 The tadpole's back legs appear later. It swims about using its tail and little back legs.

3 Next, its front legs pop out. As it feeds, the tadpole's body starts to grow.

4 As its body grows, the four-legged tadpole's tail gets smaller and smaller. It is now a proper froglet.

5 At last, the tadpole has become a tiny frog. It is just like its mother, only much smaller.

Frogs in the throat...

The male Darwin's frog swallows its tadpoles into a kind of throat pouch. When the tadpoles become froglets, he spits them out, one by one.

..and in the stomach

The stomach brooding frog swallows her eggs or tadpoles into her stomach. When they turn into froglets, they leave via mum's mouth!

Nurse frogs

When their tadpoles hatch, dart-poison frogs carry them on their backs to their nursery pool.

Caring dads

Male midwife toads carry their strings of eggs wrapped around their back legs.

Frogs with pockets

The male hip-pocket frog carries its tadpoles in pouches – one on each side of its body.

On their backs

Some female toads carry their sticky eggs on the spongy skin on their backs.